Biblical Names

The Prophetic Implications of Baby Boy Names

(Previously named Inspirational Ancient Biblical Names)

Rav Shaul B. Danyiel

ISBN: 1546610812
ISBN-13: 978-1546610816

Lion's Den Publications
Lionsden.info

DEDICATION

This book is dedicated to my wonderful wife Devorah, and my three terrific sons Yechezkiel BarShaul, Israel Aharon, and Adam Betzalel.

My wife's name Devorah means Bee in Hebrew, and she is rightly named. She is a true woman of valor according to Proverbs.

"An accomplished woman, who can find? – Far beyond pearls is her value." **(Proverbs 31:10)**

She is strong and productive like the bee. Bees produce honey, one of the sweetest things in this world. My wife is wonderful at preparing for holidays that are so sweet. I cannot think of any Hebrew name that describes her better.

My oldest son's Hebrew name is Yechezkiel (Ezekiel) and it means "God will be strong". I gave him this name with the hope that God would have a strong presence in his life.

My middle son's Hebrew name is Aharon (Aaron) and it means "Little mountain of God". It is my hope that he will grow up to be a leader in the Jewish faith.

My baby boy is Adam Betzalel, and this name means "Man in the shadow of God". As I have grown in my own spiritual life, I have seen the struggles people go through on their own spiritual journeys. So it is my hope that my youngest son will not have the sufferings that others have, as it is my prayer that he dwells in the shadow and protection of God always. Trials and tribulations will come but it is my hope that my sons never struggle with God or their faith. So I dedicate this book to my wife and sons. May they are blessed by their name and may they live up to the holiness of their names.

Rav Shaul B. Danyiel

CONTENTS

ACKNOWLEDGMENTS

I would like to thank and acknowledge my God, the creator of the universe for giving me the gift of life and the inspiration, creativity and calling to write about biblical names.

Next in the acknowledgment section is my wonderful wife. Without her support, encouragement and general partnership in life, life would overtake me and I would not be able to accomplish my mission in life.

I would like to thank my editor; she is wonderful and patient in dealing with me.

I have two creative friends, Michael Woodward-Fisher and Michael Castro, who are my sounding board for ideas. May it come to be that we find the opportunity to collaborate on other artistic works that we are planning!

Last but not least, I need to thank Kendra, the Administrative Assistant who was working in the office where I work as an auditor. When she was pregnant, she would come and ask me the meaning of certain. She went on to have the baby and she named the baby Ezra. Several years later I was thinking about writing a book on this topic, and I realized that there are many people like Kendra who are searching for a meaningful and purposeful name. Most people do not select the name of a child several years out. I did, but I am an exception. Most people only truly give consideration during the period of pregnancy. Then the parents are searching everywhere for a good name to destine their children. This is the primary audience for this book. However, this book is also great for the scholar that wants to understand the biblical stories more, or even for the convert to one of the Abrahamic faiths. So I would like to thank Kendra for letting me be part of the naming process

INTRODUCTION

What is in a name? Often times we walk around and identify people by their names, never giving thought to the name itself. When something or someone is named, that name is usually set for a lifetime.

We receive the name as a heritage. Most people did not receive a name that they wanted unless they made a legal name change later in life.

The surname is a name that is passed down from generation to generation with all family members receiving it. This does not identify the individual it identifies the family.

How parents choose the given name is determined by various cultural customs. Sometimes a person is named after a deceased family member to keep their memory alive, or a child is named after a living family member to honor that person.

However, the modern convention of naming rarely takes into consideration the meaning of a name. Even people seeking names that are a unique focus on names that sound pleasing but they rarely consider the meaning.

All that said, the name should identify what the hopes and aspirations are for the child. The name should have a meaning to the parents. A name should connect to their individual story as a parent, and a name can destine a child for greatness.

If you have ever wondered why there are so many people called, David, Frederick, George, Richard, Alexander, or Louis, to name a few examples, it is because these are powerful names. They are powerful because they are names of previous kings and rulers who made a great impact on the world. Names of successful people tend to carry on because these names become related to success.

In no other place do we find a collection of powerful names than in the Bible, therefore in this book I have chosen to categorize the ancient Hebrew biblical names according to professions that were valued by the ancient Israelites. The categories are the Patriarchs, the Angels, the Prophets, the Priests, the Kings, and the Warriors. I have also included names that are so strong they belong to the world and transcend the Hebrew language; particularly because they predate the Patriarchs, names like Adam and Noah. Finally, there are names of individuals that did not meet any of the categories but I felt they should be included because their story is powerful, and in other cases, the name's meaning is exceptionally deep. The list of names in this book is only a selection of names that appear in the Bible, it is not intended as a comprehensive list.

Join me on a journey to explore the meaning of these names. I will identify the roots of the actual word and show the compound meanings of the name. The name will be linked to a biblical verse. In understanding the meaning of the names we can arrive at a deeper understanding of the Biblical personage who carried this name.

For those looking for a great name to destine a child, this book might give you some great ideas. In the naming of a child, you will be able to have a prophecy over the child's life. To name a creature is to prophesy over the creature's life.

PRE-ABRAHAMIC NAMES

The following section analyzes names that are listed in the Bible before God made a covenant with Abraham. These are not Jewish names they are universal names. The names of these individuals tend to have a direct relationship to their narrative.

Adam (אָדָם - Adham) - means "Man"

The creation narrative in the book of Genesis features a lot of word play. This word play is seen in the name Adam. The Hebrew word for "blood" is *Dham* (דָּם) and it is red. The word for "red" is *Adhom* (אָדֹם). The word for "earth," from which Adham was formed, is *Adhamah* (אֲדָמָה), this is because the clay in the ground has a reddish hue. **(Genesis 2:7)**

The Hebrew letter *Aleph* is included to show the relationship to God since man is made in the image of God. **(Genesis 1:27)**

Cain (קַיִן - Kayin) - means "Acquired"

This name is related to the verb *Kanah* (קָנָה) which means "to acquire something."

"Now the man had known his wife Eve, and she conceived and bore Cain, saying, 'I have acquired a man with God.' " **(Genesis 4:1)**

Cain's story records the first murder ever to take place. Overcome by jealousy towards his brother Abel, Cain ambushes him, kills him and then tries to hide the sin of the murder.

"Cain spoke with his brother Abel. And it happened when they were in the field, that Cain rose up against his brother Abel and killed him." **(Genesis 4:8)**

Due to this incident, it is no surprise that we never see anyone named Cain as his first name. It carries astigmatism, and no matter how beautiful the name is it will forever be known as the name of the first murderer.

Abel (הבל- Havel) - means "Breath"

The word *Havel* (הבל) means "vapor" or "breath." It is closely related to the word *Avel* (אבל) which means "to mourn" or "lament." It could be that this name is the name God gave Moses when he wrote the Pentateuch to convey the message of the story since Abel's life was short, he was a murder victim, and he had no children of his own.

There are some theories that his name is not Hebrew but of Assyrian origin and the meaning is "his son" from the word *ablu*.

Abel offered up the best of what he had. He recognized who God was and he exemplified the quality of taking your best and giving it to God. He is recognized as righteous and his name is often associated with a righteous person.

"And additionally she bore his brother Abel. Abel became a shepherd, and Cain became a tiller of the ground. After a period of time, Cain brought an offering to God of the fruit of the ground; and as for Abel, he also brought of the firstlings of his flock and from their choicest. God turned to Abel and to his offering." **(Genesis 4:2-4)**

Seth (שֵׁת - Sheth) - means "Look alike"

There are several opinions on the meaning of this name since it can potentially be linked to several close roots. Therefore, in keeping with the idea that the meaning of the name matches the destiny and narrative of the biblical character the most likely root word is *Shava* (שׁוה) and it means "look alike." It could very well be that Seth looked like Abel so he was named Seth since Eve believed that Seth was a replacement for Abel.

"Adam knew his wife again, and she bore a son and named him Seth, because: 'God has provided me another child in the place of Abel, for Cain had killed him.' " (**Genesis 4:25**)

Alternatively, Seth could have looked just like his father Adam. It is possible that both Abel and Seth looked identical to Adam. Regardless of the differing opinions, Seth is a wonderful biblical name.

"When Adam had lived one hundred and thirty years, he begot in his likeness and his image, and he named him Seth." (**Genesis 5:3**)

Enoch (חֲנוֹךְ - Chanoch) - means "Dedicated"

The root word is *Chanak* (חָנַךְ) is a verb meaning "to dedicate" or "to inaugurate". A secondary meaning is "educated".

This man was considered to be so righteous and his relationship with God was so strong that he never physically died. He just walked off into the spiritual realm with God. Therefore, he must have been absolutely dedicated to his relationship with God.

"Enoch walked with God; then he was no more, for God had taken him." **(Genesis 5:24)**

Methuselah (מתושלח - Methushelach) - means "His death will send"

The Hebrew word for "death" is *Meth* (מת), this is followed by the possessive third-person suffix *U* (ו). The final root is the verb *Shelach* (שלח) meaning "sent." All together it gives the meaning "His death sent".

According to tradition, the great flood of Noah's time began when Methuselah died. So the deeper meaning of the name is "his death shall bring judgment." In this case, his death did bring about the judgment of the whole earth.

"Methuselah lived one hundred and eighty-two years and begot Lamech. And Methuselah lived seven hundred and eighty-two years after begetting Lamech, and he begot sons and daughters. All the days of Methuselah were nine hundred and sixty-nine years, and he died." **(Genesis 5:25-27)**

Noah (נח - Noach) - means "Rest"

This name is in its simplest form and it means "rest."

The story of Noach is found in the sixth chapter of the book of Genesis. This narrative seems to be a universal theme because every culture around the world has a deluge story.

"These are the offspring of Noah – Noah was a righteous man, perfect in his generations; Noah walked with God." **(Genesis 6:9)**

Many people think that Noah only brought two of every animal on the ark. This is a fallacy. In actuality, the scripture teaches us differently. Noah was commanded to build an ark and to place on the ark seven pairs of the clean animals and one pair of unclean kind of animals. Then there were other restrictions on which animals he was to bring on the Ark. For example, they had to be land, air-breathing animals.

"Of every clean animal take unto you seven pairs, a male with its mate, and of the animal that is not clean, two, a male and female, to keep seed alive upon the face of the earth." **(Genesis 7:2-3)**

PATRIARCHAL NAMES

The following section analyzes the names of the Patriarchs of the Jewish people. Included in this section are the names of close family members of the Patriarchs.

Abraham (אברהם - Avraham) – means "Father of many nations"

Avram (אברם) means "father," "most high," or "elevated." This is an example of a name that was actually changed by God. The letter *Hey* (ה) represents God when it is inserted properly into any name. God added the letter *Hey* (ה) changing Avram to Avraham. The scripture tells us the new meaning is "Father of many nations." Avraham is the only person that was referred to as the friend of God.

"As for Me, this is My covenant with you: You shall be a father of a multitude of nations; your name shall no longer be called Avram, but your name shall be Avraham, for I have made you the father of a multitude of nations" **(Genesis 17:4-5)**

God made a covenant with Avraham, according to Genesis chapter 15 and 17. This is why when a person converts to Judaism the title "son (or daughter) of Avraham" is added to their new name.

Avraham is the only person that was referred to as the friend of God.

Isaac (יִצְחָק -Yitzchack) – means "He will laugh (last)"

The root of the name is the verb *Tzachak* (צָחַק) which means "to laugh." We place a Hebrew character *yod* (יֹ) in front of it to conjugate the verb for the future tense third person. To give us the meaning "He will laugh last" and it is implied that he is the one who will have the last laugh at the end of the story.

Now Sarah was barren when the three messengers came to visit Abraham in Genesis 18. In verse 10, Abraham was told that Sarah would have a child by the following year. Sarah overheard the conversation and began to laugh. God asked Abraham why Sarah laughed and then confirmed that by the following year that she would have a child.

"Sarah conceived and bore a son unto Abraham in his old age, at the appointed time which God had spoken. Abraham called the name of his son who was born to him – whom Sarah had borne him – Isaac." **(Genesis 21:2)**

Ishmael (יִשְׁמָעֵאל - Yishmael) – means "God will hear"

Ishmael was not a patriarch of the Jewish people. However, he was the oldest son of Avraham and so out of respect he is included in this category.

The root is *Shema* (שְׁמַע) which means "to hear," it is conjugated for the future tense by placing the *Yod* (י) character in front of the root. Then *El* (אֵל), meaning God, is attached as a suffix forming the name Ishmael which means that "God will hear."

His mother Hagar was hiding and an angel of God found her by a well.

"The angel said to her, 'Behold, you will conceive, and give birth to a son; you shall name him Ishmael, for HaShem, has heard your prayer.' " **(Genesis 16:3-15)**

"His sons Isaac and Ishmael buried him in the cave of Machpelah, in the field of Ephron the son of Zohar the Hittite, facing Mamre." **(Genesis 25:9)**

Jacob (יעקב – Ya'acob) means "He will grab the heel"

Israel (ישראל – Yisrael) means "Wrestles with God"

This patriarch was born as *Ya'acob* (יעקב), which is a reference to him grabbing the heel, the *Akav* (עקב), of his brother.

"After that, his brother emerged with his hand grasping on to the heel of Esau; so he called his name Ya'acob" **(Genesis 25:26)**

Later on, in life, Jacob had a very spiritual encounter where it is recorded that he wrestled with an angel and then he was given the name *Yisrael* (ישראל). The verb *Sara* (שרע) means "to wrestle," and the word *El* (אל) means God. So Yisrael (ישראל) means "he will wrestle with God."

"Jacob was left alone and a man wrestled with him until the break of dawn. When he perceived that he could not overcome him, he struck the socket of his hip; so Jacob's hip socket was dislocated as he wrestled with him. Then he said, 'Let me go, for dawn has broken.' And he said, 'I will not let you go unless you bless me.' He said to him, 'What is your name?' He replied, 'Jacob.' He said, 'No longer will it be said that your name is Jacob, but Israel, for you have striven with the Divine and with man and have overcome.' "

(Genesis 32:25-29)

An alternative understanding is that *Sar* (שׂר) is "prince" so Israel (ישׂראל) also has a connotation of being a prince of God.

THE TRIBES OF ISRAEL

Israel had 12 sons who became the 12 tribes of Israel

Reuben (רובֵן – Reuven) – means "Behold a son!"

The verb is *to see* (ראה – Ra'ah), it is conjugated in the command form (רו - Reu). The word for son (בֵן- Ben) is attached to the word to indicate what we are commanded to look at. Therefore, the meaning is 'behold a son!'

Reuven was the eldest son of Jacob. He was born while Jacob was working as a shepherd for his father in law Laban.

"Leah conceived and bore a son, and she called his name Reuben, as she had declared, 'Because God has discerned my humiliation, for now, my husband will love me.' " **(Genesis 29:32)**

"Reuven, you are my firstborn, my strength and my initial vigor, foremost in rank and foremost in power." **(Genesis 49:3)**

Simeon (שמעון - Shimon) means "Little heard thing"

Shimon was the second son of Israel (Jacob) and Leah. The root is *Shema* (שמע), and the suffix "on" (ון) is the diminutive form and refers to something small.

"And she conceived again and bore a son and declared, 'Because God has heard that I am unloved, He has given me this one also,' and she called his name Simeon". **(Genesis 29:33).**

Levi (לֵוִי) – means "to attach"

The root is *lava* (לוה) which means join or be joined, or attach.

Levi was the third son of Israel (Jacob) and Leah.

This was a priestly tribe and although they were descended from Israel (Jacob) they were not one of the tribes that inherited the land.

"Again she conceived, and bore a son and declared, 'This time my husband will become attached to me for I have borne him three sons', therefore, she called his name Levi". **(Genesis 29:34)**

Judah (יְהוּדָה - Yehudah) – means "One who praises of God"

This name is formed by combining two root words. The first root is the noun *hod* (הוֹד) and it means "majesty," "glory" or "splendor." The second root is *yada* (יָדָה) which means "to praise" or "give thanks." As a name, it means "One who praises God."

"She conceived again, and bore a son and declared, 'This time let me gratefully praise God'; therefore she called his name Judah; then she stopped giving birth. **(Genesis 29:35)**

"Judah – you, your brothers shall acknowledge; your hand will be at your enemy's nape; your father's sons will prostrate themselves to you. A lion cub is Judah; from the prey, my son, you elevated yourself. He crouches, lies down like a lion, and like an awesome lion, who dares rouse him?" **(Genesis 49:8-10)**

Zebulun (זבולון - Zevulon) – means "A place of honor"

The root *zaval* (לְבָז) can mean "to honor" or "to dwell". It is a place that is set aside to honor a person. Then the diminutive form *On* (ון) is added to the root to make a name of a child.

"Then Leah conceived again and bore Jacob a sixth son. Leah said, 'God has endowed me with a good endowment; now my husband will make his permanent home with me for I have borne him six sons.' So she called his name Zebulun." **(Genesis 30:19-20)**

"Zebulun shall settle by seashores. He shall be the ship's harbor, and his last border will reach Zidon." **(Genesis 49:13)**

Issachar (יִשָּׂשכָר - Yishshachar) – means "There is a reward"

Yesh (יֵשׁ) means "there is" and this is combined with the word *Sachar* (שָׂכָר) which means reward. Together the name means "There is a reward."

"God hearkened to Leah, and she conceived and bore Jacob a fifth son. And Leah declared, 'God has granted me my reward because I gave my maidservant to my husband.' So she called his name Issachar." **(Genesis 30:17-18)**

"Issachar is a strong-boned donkey; he rests between the boundaries. He saw tranquility that it was good, and the land that it was pleasant, and he bent his shoulder to bear and he became an indentured laborer." **(Genesis 49:14)**

Dan (דן - Dhan) – means "Judge"

The name for Dan is already in the simplest root form and means judge.

Dan is the son of Bilhah and Jacob.

"So she gave him Bilhah her maidservant as a wife, and Jacob consorted with her. Bilhah conceived and bore Jacob a son. Then Rachel said, 'God had judged me, He has also heard my voice and has given me a son.' She, therefore, called his name Dan. **(Genesis 30:4-6)**

"Dan will avenge his people the tribes of Israel will be united as one. Dan will be a serpent on the highway, a viper by the path that bites horse's heels so its rider falls backward. For Your salvation do I long, O God." **(Genesis 49:16-18)**

Gad (גָּד - Ghadh) - means "Good Luck" or "Good Fortune"

The name Gad can come from one of two roots. The first root is Gadad (גָּדַד) and this means "to cut or invade." The second possible root is Gadah (גָּדָה) meaning "to cut, cut or tear away", and as you can see it is closely related to the first root.

So how is this related to luck or fortune? One idea is that it has to deal with his birth. See there was a rivalry between Jacob's two wives, and both were convinced that the one who gave Jacob the most sons would be the one that is most loved. Since Leah was Jacob's first wife she might have felt that Rachel stole Jacob from her. So by giving birth through her handmaiden Zilpah, she was able to cut or tear away the love of Jacob from Rachel and bring it back to herself, thus giving her good luck or good fortune. Interestingly, tradition teaches that Zilpah was actually a half-sister of Rachel and Leah but since her mother was a slave she had the status of a maidservant.

"When Leah saw that she had stopped giving birth, she took Zilpah her maid-servant and gave her to Jacob as a wife. Zilpah, Leah's maidservant, bore Jacob a son. And Leah declared, 'Good luck has come!' So she called his name Gad." **(Genesis 30:9-11)**

The final blessing for Gad: "Gad will recruit a regiment and it will retreat on its heel." **(Genesis 49:19)**

Asher (אָשֵׁר) – means "Richness," "happiness," or "blessedness"

Asher is already in the root form of the word and means "richness," "happiness," or "blessedness".

"Zilpah, Leah's maidservant, bore a second son to Jacob. Leah declared, 'In my good fortune! For women had deemed me fortunate!' So she called his name Asher." **(Genesis 30:12-13)**

"From Asher – his bread will have richness, and he will provide kingly delicacies." **(Genesis 49:20)**

Naphtali (נפתלי - Naftali) – means "My maneuverings"

The root of this name is *Patal* (פתל) and it means "to twist" or "contort." The Hebrew character *nun* (נ), is placed in front of the verb to show that it is the passive word. Then the Hebrew character *yod* (י) is attached to the end of the word to give it possession; in this case "my maneuvering." The image is like that of a deer that maneuvers through the forest.

"Bilhah, Rachel's maidservant, conceived again and bore Jacob a second son. And Rachel said, 'Sacred schemes have I maneuvered to equal my sister, and I have also prevailed!' And she called his name Naphtali." **(Genesis 30:7-8)**

"Naphtali is a hind let loose who delivers beautiful sayings." **(Genesis 49:21)**

Joseph (יוֹסֵף - Yosef) – means "to increase"

The root is *Yasaf* (יסף) and it means "to add" or "increase." This name reflected Rachel's hope that she would again be able to conceive and have multiple children, like her sister Leah, now that she had finally conceived and given birth.

"God remembered Rachel; God hearkened to her and He opened her womb. She conceived and bore a son, and said, 'God has taken away my disgrace.' So she called his name Joseph, saying, 'May God add on for me another son.' " **(Genesis 30:22-24)**

Now Israel loved Joseph more than all his sons since he was a child of his old age, and he made him a fine woolen tunic. **(Genesis 37:3)**

This tunic is also referred to as the coat of many colors and it was a point of jealousy that caused his brothers to sell him into slavery.

However, the selling of Joseph into slavery launched a series of events that would ultimately save the Jewish people from a famine and also all the surrounding nations of Egypt at the same time. This was accomplished when Joseph interpreted Pharaoh's dreams and was eventually granted his freedom and power as the royal viceroy of the Pharaoh.

"Pharaoh called Joseph's name Zaphenath-paneah and gave him Asenath daughter of Poti-phera, Chief of On, for a wife. Thus, Joseph emerged in charge of the land of Egypt." **(Genesis 41:45)**

"The blessings of your father surpassed the blessing of my parents to the endless bounds of the world's hills. Let them be upon Joseph's head and upon the head of the exile from his brothers." **(Genesis 49:26)**

Benjamin (בנימין - Benyamin) – means "Son of my right hand"

The word for son is *Ben* (בן), and the word for right hand is *Yamin* (ימין) thus when the two words are put together the meaning is "son of my right hand."

"They journeyed from Beth-el and there was still a stretch of land to go to Ephrath when Rachel went into labor and had difficulty in her childbirth. And it was when she had difficulty in her labor that the midwife sad to her, 'Have no fear, for this one, too, is a son for you.' And it came to pass as her soul was departing – for she died – that she called his name Ben-Oni, (Son of my suffering-בן אוני), but his father called him Benjamin." **(Genesis 35:16-18)**

"Benjamin is a predatory wolf; in the morning he will devour prey and in the evening he will distribute spoils." **(Genesis 49:27)**

Ephraim (אפרים) – means "I am fruitful"

The root is *Para* (פרה) which means to be fruitful and multiply. It is conjugated with the Hebrew character Aleph (א) which can be used in the first person form in reference to Joseph. Then the plural indicator of a noun is attached to the end in the form of *im* (ים). This makes sense because if something is fruitful it, of course, would be plural. The Aleph could also indicate that it was God that made Joseph fruitful. The Aleph is a letter commonly added to Hebrew names to show a connection with God.

This root is related to the concept of being fruitful and multiplying. This concept is first introduced in Genesis.

God blessed them and God said to them, "Be fruitful and multiply, fill the earth and subdue it; and rule over the fish of the sea, the bird of the sky, and every living thing that moves on the earth." **(Genesis 1:28)**

"And the name of the second he called Ephraim for, 'God has made me fruitful in the land of my suffering.' " **(Genesis 41:52)**

Manasseh (מנשה - Menashe) -- means "to forget"

The root of the name is *Nasha* (נשה) which means "to forget."

The Hebrew letter mem (מ) is placed in front of the verbal root to make it a noun.

"Joseph called the name of the firstborn Manasseh for, "God has made me forget all my hardship and all my father's household." **(Genesis 41:51)**

"And now your two sons who were born to you in the land of Egypt shall be mine; Ephraim and Manasseh shall be mine like Reuben and Simeon." **(Genesis 48:5)**

ANGELIC NAMES

(SHEMOT MALACHIM – שמות מלאכים)

In Hebrew, the word "angel" is *Malach* (מלאך) which means "messengers." Their primary purpose in creation is to glorify and honor God. They also have the mission to communicate with mankind. We see through scriptures that there are several times they interact with man. Some examples are the three visitors to Abraham after his circumcision, the Angel that visited Samson's parents, and the Angel that answered Daniel's prayer. The list goes on and on. Angels are not intermediates between man and God they are part of his Kingly court and as such perform duties related to carrying out the word of God. They are dispatched and return to God. Their names are associated with their mission. They are very strong and powerful name. Be careful if you give your child a name of an Angel, the Angel just might show up when you are calling your child.

Raphael (רפאל- Rafael) – means "God is a healer"

The word *Rophe* (רופה) means "healer." This angel is said to be the angel that comes to heal a person when they are sick or injured. Raphael, therefore, means "God is a healer".

In Genesis Chapter 17 Avraham had just been circumcised. He is at the peak of a painful recovery when three angels visit him. Tradition holds that the three angels were Michael, Gabriel, and Raphael. Two of the Angels go on to Sodom and Gomorrah to destroy it. Tradition varies on which angel stays with Abraham and which two go down to Sodom and Gomorrah. Since Raphael is a healing angel it is believed by some that he is the angel that stays with Avraham.

"He lifted his eyes and saw: And behold! Three men were standing over him. He perceived, so he ran toward them from the entrance of the tent and bowed toward the ground." **(Genesis 18:2)**

Michael (מיכאל) – means "Who is like God!"

The first syllable of the word is *Mi* (מי) and it means "who". The second part is *Cha* (כ) and it means "like" or "as". The last part of the name is *El* (אל) which means "God". When the three parts are put together the meaning is "Who is like God".

Now if you were confronted by a spiritual being and they were standing in front of you, and you really had no conception of God or knew very little about spirituality it would make sense that any angel could be mistaken for God. Especially, since this specific angel is regarded by many theologians as the strongest Archangel that exists. This Archangel is also held to be the national Angel associated with the children of Israel.

"But the (heavenly) prince of the Persian kingdom stood opposed to me for twenty-one days, until Michael, one of the foremost (heavenly) princes, came to help me, for I had remained there (alone) beside the kings of Persia." **(Daniel 10:13)**

"At that time Michael will stand, the great (heavenly) prince who stands in support of the members of your people, and there will be a time of trouble such as there had never been since there was a nation until that time. But at that time your people will escape; everything that is found written in this book (will occur)." **(Daniel 12:1)**

There is a possibility that Michael was one of the three angels that appeared to Abraham after his circumcision, in addition, Michael might be the angel who appeared to Samson's parents to announce that Samson would be born to his barren mother.

Gabriel (גבריאל - Gavriel) – means "Mighty warrior of God"

This name is a mighty and powerful angelic name. The word *Gever* (גבר) in Hebrew is a word for man, but it is a word that connotes a mighty warrior. The verb of *Gavar* means "to conquer." Therefore, the name Gavriel means "mighty warrior of God." This angel might actually look like a man and thus mighty man and the word of God, *El* (אל), together gives a meaning that inspires awe and would make anyone want to stay away from him.

He is not an Angel that you would want to just show up at any given time. He is related to the destruction of cities. It is possible that Gavriel and Michael are the two Angels that are related to the destruction of Sodom and Gomorrah in Genesis chapter 19.

"I heard a human voice in the middle of Ulai; he called out and said, 'Gabriel, explain the vision to that man.' " **(Daniel 8:16)**

"I was still speaking in prayer, when the man Gabriel whom I had seen in the earlier vision, was lifted in flight approaching me, at about the time of the afternoon offering." **(Daniel 9:21)**

Ariel (אריאל)– means "Lion of God." (Pronounced with a long A at the beginning of the name)

The word *Ari* (ארי) means "lion." Then *El* (אל - El), the word for God, is attached to the word Ari. This angel is the Lion of God. Strong and mighty like a Lion.

Tradition teaches that this is one of the strongest Angels there are. However, the name in relationship to an angel does not appear in scripture like Michael and Gabriel. The name as applied to a man appears once, in a recitation of genealogy from the tribe of Gad.

"Of Arod, the Arodite family; of Areli, the Arelite family." **(Numbers 26:17)**

To the Ancient mindset, a lion is patient and ferocious. He waits for the right time to strike. He is associated with a wise King.

PROPHET NAMES

(Shemot HaNavi''im - שמות הנביאים)

Moses (משה -Moshe) - means "Drew from the water"

Yekutiel (יקותיאל) - means "God will be my hope"

Moshe was a unique individual because he does not fall into any category but falls into all categories. In other words, he was not a Priest but he is the one that taught the priests how to be priests, he was not a King but he lead the whole nation like he was a King, he was said to be the father of all prophets. Since he is considered to be the father of all prophets he is at the top of our list of prophet names, even though he could easily be listed amongst the names of the Kings, Prophets or even Warriors. In fact, he was a great warrior for Egypt before he was exiled into the desert and found God.

Moses is the name given to him by the daughter of Pharaoh. The word *Moshe* (משה) is the Hebrew version of that name. The root means "draw out of the water". However, tradition maintains that his biological mother Yochaved named him Yekutiel (יקותיאל) meaning "God is my hope." This name expressed her hope and trust that God would take care of him, and return him to his people. The root of this word is *kavei* (קוה) and it means "hope." It is conjugated and the possessive first person is attached to the end and then El (אל) version of God's name is attached.

"The woman conceived and gave birth to a son. She saw that he was good and she hid him for three months. She could not hide him any longer, so she took for him a wicker basket and smeared it with clay and pitch; she placed the child into it and placed it among the reeds on the bank of the River." **(Exodus 2:2)**

"An angel of God appeared to him in a blaze of fire from amid the bush." **(Exodus 3:2)**

"God would speak to Moses face to face, as a man would speak with his fellow; then he would return to the camp. His servant, Joshua son of Nun, a lad, would not depart from within the Tent." **(Exodus 33:11)**

Eldad (אֶלְדָּד – Eldhadh) - means "God is love"

Medad (מֵידָד – Midhadh) - means "Who is love"

The root of this name is uncertain. It can either be from *Dawad* (דוד) or *Yadhadh* (ידד,) both are unclear in the meaning but by context throughout scripture, it appears to be related to love. The word *Dhadh* (דד) means "nipple" and this is related to love because of the suckling of a child to the mother. This is the same root as we see in the name of David.

"Two men remained behind in the camp, the name of one was Eldad and the name of the second was Medad, and the spirit rested upon them; they had been among the recorded ones, but they had not gone out to the Tent, and they prophesied in the camp." **(Numbers 11:26)**

Samuel (שמואל -Shmuel) - means "Request from God"

The primary meaning of the name is a combination of two words. The first word is *Shaul* (שאול) which means "requested" and the second word is *Me'el* (מאל) which means "from God".

A passage in Scripture confirms this primary meaning of the name:

"However, And it happened with the passage of the period of days that Hannah had conceived, and she gave birth to a son. She named him Samuel, for (she said), 'I requested him from God.' " **(1 Samuel 1:20)**

A possible secondary meaning, comes from a play on words, due to the way it sounds, *Shmuel* sounds like the word *Shema* (שמע) which means "hear" and the word for "God" which is *El* (אל) it appears that the meaning would be the same as the name of *Ishmael* (ישמעאל - Yishmael) which means "God hears." This would make sense since Hannah prayed for a son and one was granted to her.

God called to Samuel, and he said, "Here I am." **(1 Samuel 3:4)**

Nathan (נתן) - means "Gift of God"

The verb "to give" is *Nathan* (נתן) and as a noun, it is named that means "Gift." This is the short version of the name Nathaniel (נתניאל or נתנאל) which includes the word *El* (אל) for God.

Nathan was the prophet during the reigns of King David and King Solomon. He was the prophet that chastised King David after the incident with Bat-Sheba and he was the Prophet that helped make sure that Solomon was the next king after King David.

"Nathan then said to David, 'You are that man! Thus said God, God of Israel: 'I anointed you as king over Israel and I saved you from Saul's hand…' " **(2 Samuel 12:7)**

Elijah (אליّהוּ - Eliyahu) – means "My God is God"

Eli (אֵלי) means "my God." *Yah* (יָה) is a reference to the divine name of God. The word *Hu* (הוּ) is a pronoun for "he" since two *Hey* characters would be next to each other and since two are soft one disappears. The verb "to be" is rarely used in Hebrew but it is often implied. Therefore, the meaning of the whole name is "my God is God."

Three items of great note about Elijah is that: he openly challenged the pagans **(1 Kings 18:25),** he fled to a cave where an Angel of God meet him and feed him **(1 Kings 19:5),** and later he was caught up in a fiery chariot that God sent to take him out of this world **(2 Kings 2:11).**

In the Jewish tradition, Elijah plays a major role since it is said that his presence is at every Passover Meal and every Brit Milah (Ritual Circumcision). He has this privilege because he was the one who testified that the Jewish people were not obeying God and this are two major practices of the faith.

Elisha (אלישע) - means "My God is Salvation"

The word *Eli* (אלי) means "my God". The root *Yasha* (ישע) means "salvation". When we put them together the name becomes "My God is Salvation".

Elisha superseded Elijah as a prophet. This prophet had did amazing miracles. He raised a dead child **(2 Kings 4:35)**, parted the Jordan river just like Elijah before him **(2 Kings 2:13-14)**, and even after he had died miracles were attributed to him as a dead man was thrown into his cave and came alive when he touched the bones of Elisha. **(2 Kings 13:21).**

"And you shall anoint Jehu son of Nimshi as king over Israel, and anoint Elisha son of Shaphat from Abel-meholah as a prophet in your stead." **(1 Kings 19:16)**

Isaiah (יֶשַׁעְיָהוּ - Yeshayahu) – means "God is Salvation"

The root word of this name is *Yasha* (יֶשַׁע) which means "salvation." We put the word for God (יָהּ -Yah), and the conjugated word for "to be" and this forms the word "God is Salvation".

"The vision of Isaiah son of Amoz, which he saw concerning Judah and Jerusalem, in the days of Uzziah, Jotham, Ahaz, and Hezekiah, kings of Judah." **(Isaiah 1:1)**

Isaiah had a visionary experience, unlike most prophets. In the story of his calling, he had a vision of the heavenly court, where the Almighty was sitting on the heavenly throne and ministering angels were flying all around. Then the Seraphim angels flew and took a piece of coal from the altar to purge Isaiah's mouth.

"I heard the voice of the Lord, saying, "Whom shall I send, and who shall go for us?" And I said, "Here I am! Send me!" **(Isaiah 6:8)**

Jeremiah (ירמיהו -Yirmiyahu) - means "may God exalt"

The root is *Rum* (רום) which means "to be high." We place the 3rd person conjugate *Yod* (י) in front of the root and it means "to elevate" or "exalt," then we add the *Yah* (יה) version of the name of God, and the "to be" verb (הו) and the end resultant name is "He will exalt his God".

"The words of Jeremiah son of Hilkiah, of the Kohanim who were in Anathoth, in the land of Benjamin, to whom the word of God came in the days of Josiah son of Amon, king of Judah, in the thirteenth year of his reign. The word of God came to him in the days of Jehoiakim son of Josiah, king of Judah, until the end of the eleventh year of Zedekiah son of Josiah, king of Judah, until Jerusalem was exiled in the fifth month." **(Jeremiah 1:1-5)**

"Then God extended His hand and touched my mouth, and God said to me, 'Behold! I have placed My words in your mouth. See, I have appointed you this day over the nations and over the kingdoms, to uproot and to smash, and to destroy and to overthrow, to build and to plant.'" **(Jeremiah 1:9-10)**

Ezekiel (יחזקאל -Yechezkiel) – means "God will be strong"

The root of this name is the word *Chazak* (חזק) which means "to be strong". It is conjugated in the future tense. This tells us that someone will be strong. So the word *El* (אל) for God is attached to give the meaning that God will be strong. It is clear that God was very strong in how He dealt with Ezekiel.

"It happened in the thirtieth year, in the fourth month, on the fifth of the month, as I was among the exile by the River Chebar; the heavens opened and I saw visions of God. On the fifth of the month, which was in the fifth year of the exile of King Jehoiachin, the word of God came to Ezekiel son of Buzi, the Priest, in the land of the Chaldeans, by the River Chebar; and the hand of God came upon him there." **(Ezekiel 1:1-3)**

"He then said to me, 'Son of Man, that which you find, eat; eat this scroll then go speak to the House of Israel!' So I opened my mouth and He fed me that scroll. And He said to me, 'Son of Man, feed your stomach and fill your innards with this scroll that I give to you.' So I ate, and it was as sweet as honey in my mouth." **(Ezekiel 3:1-3)**

Hosea (הושׁע - Hoshea) - means "God is Salvation"

There are two roots that could be at play with this name. The first root is *yasha* (ישׁע) meaning "to be saved," and the second root is *shava* (שׁוע) meaning "to cry out for help" or "cry out to be saved." The difference between the two is similar to "Alas, Save" or "Alas, there is salvation." The combination of the two letters of God's name in front of the root "Salvation" can give the additional meaning of "God is Salvation."

"The word of God that came to Hosea son of Beeri in the days of Uzziah, Jotham, Ahaz and Hezekiah, the kings of Judah, and in the days of Jeroboam son of Joash, king of Israel." **(Hosea 1:1)**

Joel (יואל -Yoel) – means "God is God"

One way to refer to God in a word is to add a combination of two letters from the unpronounceable four-letter name of God. In this case, the two letters are *Yo* (יו), and they represent the God that appeared to Moses on top of Mount Sinai. The standard word for God is *El* (אל). When placed together the meaning is that the God of Moses is the true God.

"The word of God, which came to Joel son of Pethuel" **(Joel 1:1)**

"Blow the shofar in Zion and sound the trumpet on My holy mountain! Let all the inhabitants of the land tremble; for the day of God has come; it is near." **(Joel 2:1)**

Amos (עָמוֹס) – mean "The one who bears the burden."

The root means "to load" or "carry a load." This is in the simple form and cannot be broken down any further.

"The words of Amos, who was one of the herders of Tekoa, who saw visions concerning Israel in the days of Uzziah king of Judah and in the days of Jeroboam son of Joash king of Israel, two years before the earthquake." **(Amos 1:1)**

Obadiah (עובדיה -Ovadiah) – means "Servant of God"

The word *Oved* (עובד) means "servant" or "worker," and we put the *Yah* (יה) version of God's name as a suffix, and then the resulting name is Obadiah.

"The vision of Obadiah; thus said the Lord God concerning Edom" **(Obadiah 1:1)**

Jonah (יוֹנָה - Yonah) – means "Dove"

No need to look for root words in this name. In Hebrew, a dove and a pigeon are called by the same name: *Yonah*.

"And the word of God came to Jonah son of Amittai (אֲמִתַּי) saying, 'Arise! Go to Nineveh, the great city and call out against her, for their wickedness has ascended before Me.'" **(Jonah 1:1-2)**

Jonah runs away from his mission and is swallowed by a sea creature that is very much like a whale. God gives him a second chance and he then travels to Nineveh and convinces the wicked people to repent of its evils ways. Historically, it is believed that the people Nineveh worshiped a fish type god. Therefore, Jonah's testimony would have been greatly accepted by the people because Jonah's story would have resonated with the people, and we are told by the end of the story that the people did repent.

Note: The name *Amittai* (אֲמִתַּי) means "My Truth" and a variant of this name is *Emet* (אֱמֶת), and this name means "Truth".

Michah (מיכה) – means "Who is like God"

This is the same name and meaning as Michael. The difference is that the name of God is the Yah (יה) form instead of the El (אל) form of God's name.

"The word of God that came to Micah the Morashite, in the days of Jotham, Ahaz, and Hezekiah, kings of Judah – that he saw concerning Samaria and Jerusalem." **(Micah 1:1)**

Nahum (נחום - Nachum) - means "Comfort"

The root *Naham* (נחם), means "comfort." This is a shortened version of the name Nehemiah (נחמיה - Nechemiyah). The common Jewish name Menachem is a derivative form of this name.

"A prophecy regarding Nineveh. The book of the vision of Nahum the Elkoshite" **(Nahum 1:1)**

Habakkuk (חבקוק - Chavaquq) - means "Embrace"

The root means *Chavaq* (חבק) means "to embrace" or "hug."

According to Jewish tradition, he came after the prophet Nachum in a long line of prophets back to Moses. His message is that although evil exists in the world, and bad things happen to good people, the solution to the problem is that people embrace God.

"The prophecy that Habakkuk the prophet saw" **(Habakkuk 1:1)**

Zephaniah (צפניה - Tzefaniah) - means "the hidden God"

The root is *Tzafan* (צפן) which means "to hide" or "to store up." Then two letters for God's name *Yah* (יה) is attached. This brings us to the meaning "Hidden God" or even possibly "The hidden storehouse of God".

According to Jewish tradition, Zephaniah was a contemporary prophet of Jeremiah. While Jeremiah was prophesizing publicly, Zephaniah was prophesizing in the synagogue and places of worship.

"The word of God that came to Zephaniah, son of Cushi, son of Gedaliah, son of Amariah, son of Hezekiah, in the days of Josiah son of Amon, king of Judah." **(Zephaniah 1:1)**

Haggai (יָגֲּח - Chaggai) - means "My holiday"

The root is *Chug* (גוח) and it means "circle." From this concept, we get the Hebrew word for the holiday, *Chag* (גח) because it is cyclical on the calendar.

"In the second year of King Darius, in the sixth month, on the first day of the month, the word of God came by the hand of Haggai the prophet to Zerubbabel son of Shealtiel, governor of Judea, and to Joshua son of Jehozadak, the high priest, saying: 'Thus said God, Master of Legions: This nation has said, 'The time has not yet come!' But I say 'It is the time for the Temple of God to be rebuilt!' " **(Haggai 1:1)**

Zechariah (זכריה) – means "God remembers"

The root word is *Zachar* (זכר) is the verb for "to remember", and then the *Yah* (יה) form of the name of God is attached and makes the name "God remembers".

"In the eighth month, in the second year of Darius, the word of God came to Zechariah son of Berechiah son of Iddo, the prophet, saying: God became wrathful with your forefathers, wrath. Say to the people: Thus said God, Master of Legions: Return unto Me – the word of God, Master of Legions – and I will return unto you, said God, Master of Legions." **(Zechariah 1:1-3)**

Malachi (מלאכי) - means "My messenger" or "My angel"

The word *Malach* (מלאך) means "angel" or "messenger." We put the possessive *yod* (י) character to indicate that it belongs to the first person. In this case, the prophet is speaking for God and therefore, the name means "Messenger of God".

"The prophecy of the word of God to Israel, by the hand of Malachi" **(Malachi 1:1)**

Daniel (דָּנִיֵאל – Dhanyiel) – means "God is my Judge"

The word *Dan* (דָּן) means "judge," and we give it the letter *Yod* (י) which is possessive and changes the word to "my Judge." Then we explain who the judge is by adding the word *El* (אֵל) which means God.

Daniel was a young man when he was forced into the Babylonians Exile. (**Daniel 1:3-4**) However, he quickly became an advisor to the Babylonians Kings. One of the most memorable occurrences related to Daniel was when he was thrown into the lion's den because he refused to compromise his faith. Another story is when he interprets writing that miraculously appears on the wall at the Kings banquet.

Ezra (עֶזְרָא) - means "help"

The word for help is *Ezer* (עֶזֶר) and this word is not a traditional Hebrew word; it appears to be an Aramaic name based on Hebrew. This is indicated by the character Aleph (א) that appears at the end of the word.

Ezra was instrumental in the building of the second temple in Jerusalem.

"This Ezra ascended from Babylonia; he was a brilliant scholar of the Law of Moses, which God, God of Israel, had given. The king granted him his every request, according to the command of God, His God, to him." **(Ezra 7:6)**

PRIESTLY NAMES

Image of the High Priest (HaCohen HaGadol)

(הכהן הגדול)

Malchizedek (מלכי-צדק – Melchi-Tzedheq) - means "Righteous King"

The word *Melech* (מלך) means "King" and the word *Tzedek* (צדק) means "righteousness," and when we place these two words together is means "Righteous King." This might not have been an actual name but rather a title of the King.

But Malchizedek, King of Salem, brought out bread and wine; he was a priest of God, the Most High. **(Genesis 14:18)**

Jethro (יתרו - Yithro) means "more or abundance"

Reuel (רעואל) means "friend of God"

The root is *yatar* (יתר) and it means "more." He also was referred to by the name Reuel.

The root is *ra'a* (רעה) this means "a friend" or "associate." Then you put the *El* (אל) form of God's name and you have a name that means "Friend of God".

He was not a priest like Malchizedek or from the Aaronic priestly line. He was actually a polytheistic priest and worshiped multiple gods. He was the father-in-law of Moses. However, when he heard of all the great things that God had done for the Jewish people in bringing them out of the land of Israel he converted from his polytheistic beliefs and followed the God of Moses, and became an advisor for Moses **(Exodus 18:17-23).**

"Now I know that God is greater than all the gods" **(Exodus 18:11)**

Aaron (אהרון - Aharon) – means "God's little mountain"

Aharon was the first High Priest (Kohen Gadol) for the Israelites.

The word *har* (הר) means "mountain." The *on* (ון) is a diminutive, and when it is attached to *har* (הר) it becomes "little mountain." The letter Aleph (א) means strength in the ancient pictorial form of paleo-Hebrew and sometimes it is a symbol for God when it appears in a name where it has no other purpose. In this name, where the Aleph character does not serve a purpose, it is easy to see that it was added as a reference to God. Therefore, the name means "God's little mountain"

Nadav (נדב – Nadhav) – means "to be noble, generous or willing"

Abihu (אביהוא – Avihu) – means "He is my Father" (God is my father)

The Bible does not much mention a lot of details regarding these two brothers. They are listed here together because their story is closely interrelated.

The root word *Nadav* (נדב) means "call," "to impel," "incite," "to be willing," "noble" or "generous." We can see that he was very zealous or willing to serve in the tabernacle the only problem is that he served in a manner that God did not call for him to serve in.

The name Abihu (אביהוא) is a name with a few words in it. The first is *Avi* (אבי) meaning "my father", and the next word is *hu* (הוא) the word for "He". When placed together it means "He is my father"; like so many Hebrew names it is an allusion is to God.

"These are the names of the sons of Aaron, the firstborn was Nadab, and Abihu, Elazar, and Ithamar. **(Numbers 3:2)**

"A fire comes forth from before God and consumed them, and they died before God." **(Leviticus 10:2)**

Ithamar (איתמר – Eethamar) – means "Island of Palms"

The word *Ee* (אי) means "island." The word *tamar* (תמר) means "palm tree." When placed together it is "Island of Palms."

Ithamar was one of the four sons of Aaron the high priest. He was a priest himself but was not the high priest. After the death of Aaron, the mantle of high priest fell upon Eliezer.

"These were the names of the sons of Aaron; the firstborn was Nadav, and Abihu, Elazar, and Ithamar. These were the names of the sons of Aaron, the anointed Priest, whom he inaugurated to minister. Nadav and Abihu died before God when they offered an alien fire before God in the wilderness of Sinai, and they had no children; But Elazar and Ithamar ministered during the lifetime of Aaron, their father." **(Numbers 3:2-3:4)**

"These were the reckonings of the Tabernacle, the Tabernacle of Testimony, which was reckoned at Moses' bidding. The labor of the Levites was under the authority of Ithamar, son of Aaron the Kohen." **(Exodus 38:21)**

Elazar (אלִיעֶזֶר - Eliezer) - means "My God is my help"

First, we start with the *El* (אל) version of God's name and then we add a possessive *Yod* (י) which would make it mean "my God," and then we add the word *Azar* (עֶזֶר) which means "help" or "support to the word." This brings the name to mean "My God is helping".

"Now you, bring near to yourself Aaron your brother, and his sons with him, from among the children of Israel – Aaron, Nadab and Abihu, Elazar and Ithamar, the sons of Aaron your brother, for glory and splendor." **(Exodus 28:1)**

"Elazar son of Aaron died, and they buried him in the Hill of Phinehas his son, which was given to him on Mount Ephraim." **(Joshua 24:33)**

Zadok (צָדוֹק - Tzadhok) - means "Righteous"

The root of the name is *Tzadhek* (צדק) and it means "to be just" or "righteous."

There are several occurrences of this name in scripture:

Zadok son of Ahitub and Ahimelech son of Ebiathar were Kohanim (Priests); Seraiah was the scribe; **(2 Samuel 8:17)**

So Zadok and Abiathar returned the Ark of God to Jerusalem, and they stayed there. **(2 Samuel 15:29)**

(For further references to people with the name Zadok see **1 Kings 1:8**, **34-40**, **2:35**, **4:4**, **1 Chronicles 18:16**)

Phinehas (פִּינְחָס - Pinchas) - means "To turn to seek refuge" or the "Mouth of enchantment".

The name is a difficult one to de-code. This is a very rich name and without knowing the birth story it would be hard to know for sure.

There are two possible means of this name. The first meaning comes from combining the word *Pana* (פָּנָה), which means "to turn," with the word *Hasa* (חָסָה) which means "to seek refuge," and we drop of the final "ah" sound to make it masculine. This would make the first meaning of the word "To turn to seek refuge".

There is also an element of wordplay with this name because the Hebrew character *Samach* (ס) could be substituted for the character *Sin* (שׂ) because both have an "S" sound. It would change the meaning of the name. It could then mean two different words *Pay* (פִּי) which means "mouth" and *Nachas* (נָחָשׁ) which means "snake," "enchantment" or even "cooper."

"Phinehas son of Elazar son of Aaron the Kohen, turned back My wrath from upon the Children of Israel when he zealously avenged My vengeance among them, so I did not consume the Children of Israel in My vengeance. Therefore, say: Behold! I give him My covenant of peace." **(Numbers 25:11-12)**

Gershom (גרשום - Gershom) – means "Stranger there"

Gershom was the son of Moses. The name is a combination of two words. The first word is *Ger* (גר) which means "stranger." The second word is *Sham* (שם) which means "there." When both words are put together the form there is a shift in the vowel sound from Sham to Shom. The new name is Gershom which means "Stranger there."

She gave birth to a son and he named him Gershom, for he said, "I have been a stranger in a foreign land." **(Exodus 2:22)**

NAMES OF KINGS

(Shemot Melechim - שמות מלכים)

Saul (שָׁאוּל - Shaul) – means "Asked or borrowed (from God)"

The root of this name is a verb meaning "to ask" or "to borrow." The story is that the children of Israel asked or requested from God that they are allowed to have a King. God heard their prayer and granted them the first King of Israel and it was Shaul.

"He had a son named Saul who was exceptional and goodly; no one in Israel was more handsome than he, from his shoulders up, he was taller than any of the people." **(1 Samuel 9:2)**

However, beware of the name Shaul (שָׁאוּל), in Hebrew, it is closely related to the word for *Sheol* (לֹאִשׁ) which means "the pit" or "hell." Another closely related word is *Shual* (שׁוּעָל) which is the word for "fox." It has a different root but the sounds are very similar. In order for Shaul to have a great life he, has to outsmart the pit by thinking like a fox.

"And it happened that whenever the spirit of melancholy from God was upon Saul, David would take the harp and play with his hand, and Saul would feel relieved and it would be well with him, and the spirit of melancholy would depart from him." **(1 Samuel 16:23)**

David (דוד – Dhavidh) – means "Beloved" (By God)

Since this is a three letter root there is no way to simplify the word further. It means "beloved," and the implication is that David was beloved by God.

David is one of the largest characters in the scripture. He is the King beloved by God because of his repentant heart. Yes, he made a lot of mistakes in his life but he was humble and he always directed his heart full of repentance upon God. His rise to fame was when he slew the giant Goliath. He was the King that was one with his people, he was the King that wrote and played beautiful music and most of the Psalms. He was the warrior King and the Poet King at the same time. He is the most respected King of Jewish history and one of the most respected Kings of all human existence.

"All the tribes of Israel came to David in Hebron and spoke, saying 'Behold, we are your bone and your flesh. Even yesterday and before yesterday, when Saul was king over us, you were the one who brought Israel out and brought them in; and God had said to you, 'You shall shepherd My people Israel and you shall be ruler over Israel.' All the elders of Israel came to the King at Hebron, and King David sealed a covenant with them in Hebron before God, and they anointed David as King over Israel." **(2 Samuel 5:1)**

Salomon/Solomon (שלמה - Shlomo) – means "His peace"

The root is root *shalem* (שלם) which means "whole" or "complete." It is related to the concept of peace. To be at peace is to be whole. However, the meaning of the name is based on how it is pronounced. Shalom means peace (and also stands as a Hebrew name). For this name, we take the word for Shalom and add a suffix of "o" (ו). This suffix means "his". So the name means "his peace." Whose peace? The child is peace for the father. In this case, it means that Shlomo is the peace for his father David. However, at the same time, it has the letter hey (ה) at the end which can indicate that the peace comes from God.

It should be noted that Shlomo was really the only King of Israel that really had a united and peaceful kingdom for the most part.

The story of Shlomo: He was David's peace because David had blood on his hands as a warrior King and therefore God would not allow David to build the temple in Jerusalem. Shlomo was allowed to build the temple in Jerusalem because he was not a warrior.

Zedekiah (צדקיהו- Tzedkiyahu) - means "God is my Righteousness"

The first part of the name is *Tzedek* (צדק) which means "just" or "righteous." Then we add the Yah (יה) form of the name of God, and the *hu* (הו) which indicates the verb "is". Then the whole meaning of the name becomes "God is my Righteousness".

The name is wonderful in meaning however he was not a good king. He was the last king of ancient Israel. His children were slaughtered, he was blinded and lead into captivity.

"They seized the king and brought him up to the king of Babylonia at Riblah, in the land of Hamath, and he spoke words of judgment to him." **(Jer 52:9)**

NAMES OF WARRIORS

The following names are mostly from the times of what are often translated as the judges. However, a more accurate translation would be tribal chieftains; this was a time before there were kings that were ruling from a centralized area.

Joshua (יהושע - Yahushua) – means "God is salvation"

The basic root is either *yasha* (ישע) which means "to be delivered" or "to be saved," or the root *shava* (שוע) which means "to cry out for help." We add a conjugated form of the Yah (יה) version of God's name to the front of the word and together it forms the meaning "God is salvation."

Joshua was the famous successor of Moses (Moshe). He was one of the twelve spies that Moshe sent to spy out the land of Canaan. When the twelve came back only Joshua and Caleb were confident about conquering the land of Canaan **(Numbers 13).**

Later, after the death of Moshe, the mantle of leadership was transferred to Joshua. It is said that Moshe was like the Sun and Joshua the moon. **(Deuteronomy 34:9)**

So it is rather coincidental that the first city that was conquered under Joshua was Jericho (Yirecho meaning "its moon"). The city was conquered by marching around it seven times and blowing Trumpets also called a Shofar (which is a Ram's Horn) **(Joshua 6).**

Caleb (כָּלֵב - Khalev) - means "like the heart" or "wholehearted"

In the Hebrew language, there are animal names that appear quite often, for example, it is common for there to be names like *Ze'ev* (זְאֵב) which means "wolf," *Dov* (דוֹב) which means "bear" or *Tzvi* (צְבִי) which means "deer." So it would be easy to mix up the name Kalev with the word for "dog" which is *Kelev*. The first vowel is what makes the difference. The word for heart is *Lev* (לֵב) and the prefix of the *kaph* (כ) means "like" or "as."

One is not named after the other, even though they share some commonalities. A dog is a faithful creature to his master. Caleb was a faithful servant of God. To call him a dog because of this similarity, would be a misunderstanding and would be an insult.

Kalev was the spy faithfully in agreement, that is to say, he was wholeheartedly in agreement, with Joshua about conquering the land of Canaan while the other ten spies lacked faith that God would provide the victory for conquering the Promised Land. **(Numbers 13)**

Not

Othniel (עתניאל) - means "Strength of God"

This is a difficult name to break apart. Many sources list this as "lion of God," or "strength of God." However, I do not see how this meaning can be derived from the word. The root is not easily discernable in Hebrew. So for this name we are left with what tradition passes down as the meaning.

After the death of Joshua and before the establishment of a King, the children of Israel did not have a leader. When difficult times happened they cried out to God for a leader and God would provide them a tribal chieftain referred to as a *Shofet*. This is translated into English as a "judge." The first judge over Israel was *Othniel* (עתניאל) the brother of Caleb (כלב).

"The children of Israel cried out to God, and God set up a savior for the children of Israel and he saved them: Othniel (עתניאל) son of Kenaz (קנז), Caleb's younger brother." **(Judges 3:9-11)**

"Othniel (עתניאל) son of Kenaz (קנז), brother of Caleb (כלב), conquered it; so he gave him his daughter Achsah (עכסה) as a wife." **(Joshua 15:17)**

Ehud (אהוד) - means "I will praise"

The root for this name is Hod (הוד) and it means "majesty" or "honor." Conjugated as a verb it means "I will praise."

"The Children of Israel cried out to God, and God sent up a savior for them: Ehud son of Gera, a Benjaminite, a man with a withered right hand."(Judges 3:15)

Here we see a play on words since the name *Benjamin* (בנימין) means "Son of my right hand", and Ehud (a Benjaminite) had a withered right hand.

The story of Ehud is that he entered the chamber of Eglon the King who was oppressing the Jews while he was relieving himself. He stabbed Eglon in the stomach as he was sitting on the chair. Eglon was said to be so obese that when he was stabbed the sword went into him all the way to the hilt of the sword, that Ehud could not bring it out. Then Ehud locked the door behind him and escaped through the sewer system. **(Judges 3:15-26)**

Barak (בָּרָק – Baraq) – means "Lightning"

There is no need to break down the parts of this name because it is already in the simplest form of the word.

"She sent and summoned Barak son of Abinoam of Kedesh-Naphtali and said to him, "Behold, God, the God of Israel, has commanded, 'Go and convince the people to go toward Mount Tabor, and take with you ten thousand men from the children of Naphtali and from the children of Zebulun! I will draw toward you – to Kishon Brook – Sisera, the general of Jabin's army, with his chariot and his multitude; and I shall deliver him into your hand.' " **(Judges 4:6-7)**

Deborah said to Barak, "Arise! For this day when God has delivered Sisera into your hand – behold, god has gone forth before you!" **(Judges 4:14)**

He was a true warrior of God. God went before him. A warrior is only a true warrior for God if God is actually going before him in battle.

Gideon (גִּדְעוֹן - Gideyon) – means "The little one that cuts down," or, possibly from the sound of the name, it means "little goat."

The root is *Gidea* (גדע) and it means "to hew down" or "to cut off". This is quite appropriate for a warrior.

"An angel of God came and sat under the elm tree in Ophrah that belonged to Joash the Abi-ezrite. His son Gideon was threshing wheat at the winepress, to hide it from Midian. The angel of God appeared to him, and said to him, 'God is with you, O mighty hero!'" **(Judges 6:11-12)**

There is a possible secondary meaning based on the sound of the name. A kid is a baby goat, and in Hebrew, it is called "Gid" (גד). In fact, this might the source for the English word kid. The *on* suffix attached to the word *Gid* characterizes the diminutive form. Therefore, Gideon means a "little goat or little kid." This idea carries the image of a stubborn immovable kid.

Samson (שִׁמְשׁוֹן - Shimson) - means "Little Sun"

The word *Shemesh* (שֶׁמֶשׁ) means "Sun" and this is the root of the name Shimson. The suffix of *on* (וֹן) is a diminutive and when attached to the word *Shemesh* its meaning becomes "little sun." The sun is a very powerful creation of God. It is also one of the most misunderstood things in all of the creation. We cannot come close to it to really investigate it. It is a name one will want to give to a son if they are hoping to have a child that will grow up to be a powerhouse, a warrior or a great athlete.

"The woman gave birth to a son, and she called his name Samson; the lad grew and God blessed him." **(Judges 13:24)**

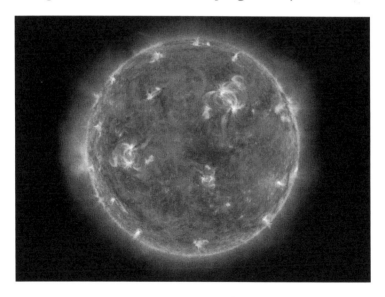

Abner (אבנר - Avner) – means "Father of light"

Av (אב) means "father," and *ner* (נר) means "light." Therefore, Avner means "father of light." It can be a reference to God since God is the father and creator of all things especially light and mentioned in Genesis.

He was the commander of the Army of King Saul and Ishbosheth. Ishbosheth was a rival of King David who was trying to establish King that was rivaling to be King of Israel right after Saul died as King David was trying to establish himself.) However, after about two years Avner rallies Israel behind King David.

"Now Abner son of Ner, the commander of Saul's army, had taken Ishbosheth the son of Saul and brought him across to Mahanaim, and made him king over Gilead, over the Asherite, over Jezreel, over Ephraim, over Benjamin and over all of Israel. Ishbosheth the son of Shaul was forty years old when he reigned over Israel, and he reigned for two years. However, the House of Judah in Hebron was loyal to David." **(2 Samuel 2:8-10)**

"Abner's message had been sent to all the elders of Israel, saying, "From yesterday and before yesterday you wanted David as king over you; so now do it! For God has said of David, 'By the hand of My servant David I shall save My people Israel from the hand of the Philistines and from the hand of all their enemies' ". **(2 Samuel 3:17)**

Uriah (אוריה) - means "light of God"

If we take the word *Or* (אור) means "light;" and could also be pronounced as *Ur*. The second part of the name is formed with two letters of God's Holy name: "Yah" (יה). The two parts combined results with the name Uriah, which is very similar in meaning to Avner (אבנר).

He was the husband of Bathsheva (בת שבע) before she married David. He was a great warrior who was obedient to his King's request. He is listed amongst David's leading warriors in **I Chronicles 11:41**.

"David sent to inquire about a woman, and someone said, 'Is this not Bath-Sheba daughter of Eliam, the wife of Uriah the Hittite?' " **(2 Samuel 11:3)**

"So it was that when Joab was besieging the city, he stationed Uriah in a place where he knew that the powerful warriors were. The men of the city came out and fought against Joab, and some people from among David's servants fell, and Uriah the Hittite also died." **(2 Samuel 11:16-17)**

Uzziel (עוזיאל) - means "God is my strength"

The root is *Uz* (עוז) which means "strength," "power" and possibly "courage." We add the *Yod* (י) to give it possession, and we add *El* (אל) meaning "God." The result is the name Uzziel (עוזיאל) which means "God is my strength".

"Also, some of them – the sons of Simeon – five hundred men, went to Mount Seir, with Pelatiah, Neariah, Rephaiah and Uzziel, the sons of Ishi, at their head. They smote the remnant of the Amalekites who had survived and dwell there, up to this day." **(1 Chronicles 4:42-43).**

OTHER NOTABLE NAMES

These are names that are not easily classified within the categories of Patriarchs, Prophets, Priests, Kings or Warriors. However, they are very important in order to move the biblical stories forward.

Perez (פֶּרֶץ - Peretz) - means "burst forth"

The name is in the simplest form already, however, it also means "explosive."

Perez is the son of Tamar and Judah. She was carrying twins. Now in the Middle East, the birth of the firstborn is very significant and carries a lot of weight in the family.

"And it happened that as she gave birth, one put out a hand; the midwife took a crimson thread and tied it on this hand saying, "This one emerged first!" And it was, as he drew back his hand, that behold! His brother emerged. And she said, "With what strength you asserted yourself!" And he called his name Perez. Afterward, his brother on whose hand was the crimson thread came out, and he called his name Zerah." **(Genesis 38:28-30)**

Zerah (זרח - Zerach) is in the simplest form and it means "to arise," or "to shine" and it is the verb associated with the sun.

This becomes a common last name in Spanish of Perez and then later Alvarez because of the Golden Age of Spain during which Jewish, Christians, and Muslim peacefully studied together.

The three in the fiery furnace

Since the three names are intimately linked to the same event it is reasonable to group them together.

Hananiah (חנניה - Chananiyah) - means "God's grace"

This name is made up of two words. The root for this name is *Chen* (חן) which means "grace." The second word is the Yah (יה) form of God's name.

Mishael (מישאל) - means "Who requested of God"

This name is composed of two words. The first word is *Mi* (מי) which means "Who", and the second word is *Sha'al* (שאל) which means "to request" or "to ask". It is implied that the request is directed to God.

Azariah (עזריה) means "God is my help"

The root is *Azar* (עזר) which means "to help," then the Yah (יה) form of God's name is added at the end.

"Among them were, from the children of Judah: Daniel, Hananiah, Mishael, and Azariah. The chief officer gave them names: to Daniel, he gave the name Belteshazzar, to Hananiah, Shadrach; to Mishael, Meshach; and to Azariah, Abednego." **(Daniel 1:6)**

"They refused to bow to the golden idol and were thrown into the fiery furnace for their faith." **(Daniel 3:13-32)**

Betzalel (בצלאל) - means "in the Shadow of God"

The word *Tzal* (צל) means "Shadow," the word *El* (אל) means "God," and when the prefix *Beit* (ב) is added then the name means "in the Shadow of God." The meaning is so significant to me that I gave this name to one of my sons. Adham Betzalel means "Man in the Shadow of God" and it is my hope and prayer that my son will be a man that is kept under the protective shadow of God.

The nickname for a child named Betzalel is *Tzali* (צלי) which means "My Shadow". So it is appropriate for a parent to call the child my shadow. One can even playfully joke with the child and call him the onion of God since *Betzal* (בצל) is the word for onion. In the Bible, Betzalel was a young teenager who was also the master craftsman of God's Tabernacle, hence this name is closely associated with creativity.

"God called him by name to be the builder because God blessed him with a Godly spirit, with wisdom, insight, and knowledge, and with every craft." **(Exodus 31:1-5, also see Exodus 35:30-35)**

Ohaliav (אָהֳלִיאָב) - means "My father's tent" or "My primary tent"

Ohel (אוֹהֵל) means "tent," and *Av* (אָב) means "father." *Av* also means God. When both root words are combined the name means "primary tent." It is important to understand that the word *Av* is related to the idea of a lineage, specifically the beginning or head of that lineage.

It is interesting to note that this man was instrumental in building the Tabernacle which was the first prototype of the Temple later built by Solomon. It was followed by two temples and the hope is that there will be a third temple in the future.

Ohaliav is called out by God to have a role in building the tabernacle with Betzalel.

(Exodus 31:1-5, see also Exodus 35:30-35 and Exodus 38:22)

Jesse (יַשַׁי - Yishai) - means "There is a God" or "My Gift"

This name is difficult to translate because the root is hard to identify since there is no Biblical narrative specifically related to Jesse. However, one opinion is that the name comes from a combination of two Hebrew words: *Yesh* (שׁ) which means "there is," and the letter *Yod* (י) which is a character often used to represent God in a name. When placed together the name means "there is a God".

Alternatively, the name *Shai* (שׁי) means "gift" so the name Jesse could also mean "Gift of God".

"The neighborhood women gave him a name, saying, 'A son is born to Naomi.' They named him Obed; he was the father of Jesse, the father of David." **(Ruth 4:17)** **Note that** the child was actually born to Ruth but Naomi raised the child as her own.

"And Obed begot Jesse, and Jesse begot David." **(Ruth 4:22)**

God said to Samuel, 'How long will you mourn over Saul when I have rejected him from reigning over Israel? Fill your horn with oil and go forth – I shall send you to Jesse the Bethlemite, for I have seen a king for Myself among his sons.' " **(1 Samuel 16:1)**

Boaz (בֹּעַז) - means "In strength" or "With courage".

The root for the name Boaz is the same as for Uzziel. The *Beit* (בּ) character means "in" or "with". When placed in front of the root *Uz* (עֹז) (which means "strength,") it gives the meaning "with strength," "with power" or "with courage." Boaz was the great-grandfather of King David.

"Naomi had a relative through her husband, a man of substance, from the family of Elimelech; his name was Boaz." **(Ruth 2:1)**

"And, what is more, I have also acquired Ruth the Moabite, the wife of Machlon, as my wife, to perpetuate the name of the deceased on his inheritance, that the name of the deceased not be cut off from among his brethren, and from the gate of his place. You are witnesses today." **(Ruth 4:10)**

"And so, Boaz took Ruth and she became his wife; and he came to her, God let her conceive, and she bore a son." **(Ruth 4:13)** The child referred to in this verse was Obed. Obed was the father of Jesse, and Jesse was the father of King David.

Absalom – (אבשלום - Avshalom) - means "Father's peace"

The root word is *Shalom* (שלום) which means "peace." The word *Av* (אב) means "father." The two words together mean "father's peace."

Absalom was King David's son. Based on the names of his sons it seems that David, as a warrior king, really longed for peace. He gave two of his son's names that are related to peace. One was *Avshalom* (אבשלום) meaning "father's peace" and the other was the famous Solomon (שלמה - Shlomo) which means "his peace."

"There was no one in all of Israel as praiseworthy for his beauty as Absalom; from the bottom of his foot to the top of his head there was no blemish in him." **(2 Samuel 14:25)**

Jonathan (יונתן – Yonathan) means "God gave" or "Gift of God"

The root of the name is the verb *Nathan* (נתן) which means "to give." The letters *Yod* (י) and the *Vav* (ו) are added at the beginning to associate the root with God. These two letters are part of the four-letter Divine name that the High Priest would only say once a year in the Temple on the Most Holy Day of Atonement (Yom Kippur - יום כיפור)

Jonathan was the son of Saul and he was the best friend and brother-in-law of David. He was always trying to keep the peace between his father and his best friend. This was a challenge since Saul was angry that the Prophet Samuel already decreed that David would be the new king after him, not Jonathan.

"So Jonathan called David, and Jonathan told him all these things. Jonathan brought David to Saul and he was before him as he had been yesterday and before." **(1 Samuel 19:7)**

Zerubbabel (זרובבל) - means "Seed of Babylon"

The word *Zera* (זרע) means "seed," and the word *Bavel* (בבל) means "Babylon." When these two words are brought together we have the name Zerubbabel. The name is meant to indicate that this individual was born in Babylon.

"Then Yeshua (ישוע) son of Yozadak (יוצדק) arose, along with his brethren the Priests (כהנים - Kohanim) and Zerubbabel (זרובבל) son of Shealtiel (שאלתיאל) and his brethren, and they built the Altar of the God of Israel, to offer burnt-offerings upon it, as is written in the Torah of Moses, the man of God." **(Ezra 3:2)**

"Then Zerubbabel son of Shealtiel and Yeshua son of Yozadak arose and began to build the Temple of God that was in Jerusalem, and with them were the prophets of God, assisting them." **(Ezra 5:2)**

CONCLUSION

In the beginning, God spoke the Universe into existence. God said, "Let there be light," and there was light **(Genesis 1:3)**. From this, we see the power of speech and specifically the power of calling something out, and the power of giving a name to something.

Now with all the Majesty and Honor due to the Ultimate King and Father of all creation, we are blessed because the King allows each and every human the possibility of participating in this aspect of creation. He allowed Adam to name each creature in this world.

"Now, the Lord God had formed out of the ground every beast of the field and every bird of the sky, and brought them to the man to see what he would call each one; and whatever the man called each living creature, that remained its name." **(Genesis 2:19)**

To give personal names then becomes a holy act. An act that should not be taken lightly. God named Adam and gave a new name to a few others, but mostly He leaves the duty of assigning names to the average person. A lot of thought and consideration should be involved in the naming process. It is an act of prophecy to destine a child.

Three entities are involved in the creation of a child: the father who provides the seed, the mother who nurtures the child in the womb, and the hidden creative power of God. The naming of a child, whether in a ceremony or not, is the peak of the whole process of bringing a child into this world. For this reason, many cultures have a naming ceremony; this is definitely the case with Judaism. So I pray that before anyone names a child, and destines the child with a prophecy, that they thoughtfully and prayerfully consider the name. And I hope that they take pleasure in naming their child, for it is a prophetic experience.

APPENDIX

Name	Hebrew & Pronunciation	Meaning	Page
Aaron	Aharon – אהרון	God's little mountain	66
Abel	Havel - הבל	Breath or Vapor	6
Abihu	Avihu – אביהוא	He is my father (God is my father)	67
Abner	Avner – אבנר	Father of light	86
Abraham	Avraham – אברהם	Father of many nations	12
Absalom	Avshalom – אבשלום	Father's peace	96
Adam	Adham – אדם	Man	4
Amittai	Amittai – אמתי	My truth	53
Amos	Amos – עמוס	The one who bears the burden	51
Ariel	Ariel – אריאל	Lion of God	37
Asher	Asher – אשר	Richness, happiness or blessedness	26
Azariah	Azariah – עזריה	God is my help	91
Barak	Baraq – ברק	Lightning	83
Benjamin	Benyamin – בנימין	Son of my right hand	29
Betzalel	Betzalel – בצלאל	In the shadow of God	92
Boaz	Boaz – בועז	In strength or with courage	95
Cain	Kayin – קין	Acquired	5
Caleb	Khalev – כלב	Like the heart or wholehearted	80
Dan	Dhan - דן	Judge	24
Daniel	Dhanyiel – דניאל	God is my Judge	61
David	Dhavidh – דוד	Beloved (By God)	75
Ehud	Ehud – אהוד	I will praise	82
Elazar	Eliezer – אליעזר	My God is my help	69
Eldad	Eldhadh – אלדד	God is love	41
Elijah	Eliyahu - אליהו	My God is God	44

Elisha	Elisha – אלישע	My God is Salvation	45
Emet	Emeth – אמת	Truth	53
Enoch	Chanoch – חנוך	Dedicated or Educated	8
Ephraim	Ephraim – אפרים	I am fruitful	30
Ezekiel	Yechezkiel– יחזקאל	God will be strong	48
Ezra	Ezra – עזרא	Help	62
Gabriel	Gavriel – גבריאל	Mighty warrior of God	36
Gad	Ghadh – גד	Good luck or Good fortune	25
Gershom	Gershom – גרשום	Stranger there	72
Gideon	Gideyon – גדעון	The little one that cuts down	84
Habakkuk	Chavaquq – חבקוק	Embrace	56
Haggai	Chaggai – חגי	My holiday	58
Hananiah	Chananiyah – חנניה	God's Grace	91
Hosea	Hoshea – הושע	God is Salvation	49
Isaac	Yitzchack– יצחק	He will laugh (last)	13
Isaiah	Yeshayahu – ישעיהו	God is Salvation	46
Ishmael	Yishmael – ישמעאל	God will hear	14
Israel	Yisrael – ישראל	Wrestles with God	15
Issachar	Yishshachar – יששכר	There is a reward	23
Ithamar	Eethamar – איתמר	Island of Palms	68
Jacob	Ya'acob – יעקב	He will grab the heel	15
Jeremiah	Yirmiyahu– ירמיהו	May God exalt	47
Jesse	Yishai – ישי	My Gift	94
Jethro	Yithro – יתרו	More or abundance	65
Joel	Yoel– יואל	God is God	50
Jonathan	Yonathan – יונתן	God gave or Gift of God	97
Joseph	Yosef – יוסף	To increase	28
Joshua	Yahushua – יהושע	God is salvation	79
Judah	Yehudah – יהודה	One who praises of God	21
Levi	Levi – לוי	To attach	20
Malachi	Malachi – מלאכי	My messenger or my angel	60

	Melchi- מלכי-צדק		
Malchizedek	Tzedheq	Righteous king	64
Manasseh	Menashe - מנשה	to forget	31
Methuselah	מתושלח - Methushelach	His death will send	9
Michael	Michael - מיכאל	Who is like God!	35
Michah	Michah - מיכה	Who is like God	54
Midad	Midhadh – מידד	Who is love	41
Mishael	Mishael - מישאל	Who requested of God	91
Moses	Moshe- משה	Drew from the water	39
Nadav	Nadhav – נדב	To be noble, generous or willing	67
Nahum	Nachum - נחום	Comfort	55
Naphtali	Naftali - נפתלי	My maneuverings	27
Nathan	Nathan - נתן	Gift of God	43
Nathaniel	Nathaniel - נתניאל	Gift of God	43
Noah	Noach - נח	Rest	10
Obadiah	Ovadiah-עובדיה	Servant of God	52
Ohaliav	Ohaliav - אהליאב	My tent is primary	93
Othniel	Othniel - עתניאל	Strength of God	81
Perez	Peretz - פרץ	Burst forth	90
Phinehas	Pinchas - פנחס	To turn to seek refuge or the mouth of enchantment	71
Raphael	Rafael - רפאל	God is a healer	34
Reuben	Reuven – רובן	Behold a son!	18
Reuel	Reuel - רעואל	Friend of God	65
Salomon	Shlomo - שלמה	His peace	76
Samson	Shimson - שמשון	Little Sun	85
Samuel	Shmuel- שמואל	Request from God	42
Saul	Shaul - שאול	Asked or borrowed (from God)	74
Seth	Sheth - שת	Look-alike	7
Simeon	Shimon – שמעון	Little heard thing	19
Uriah	Uriah - אוריה	Light of God	87
Uzziel	Uzziel - עוזיאל	God is my strength	88
Yekutiel	Yekutiel - יקותיאל	God will be my hope	39
Yonah	Yonah - יונה	Dove or Pidgeon	53

Zadok	Tzadhok – צדוק	Righteous	70
Zebulun	Zevulon – זבולון	A place of honor	22
Zechariah	Zechariah – זכריה	God remembers	59
Zedekiah	Tzedkiyahu -צדקיהו	God is my Righteousness	77
Zephaniah	Tzefaniah – צפניה	Hidden God	57
Zerah	Zerach – זרח	To arise, or to shine	90
Zerrubabel	Zerrubabel – זרובבל	Seed of Babylon	98

Rav Shaul B. Danyiel

ABOUT THE AUTHOR

Upon graduation from High School, Shaul Danyiel entered the US Army as an Infantry Paratrooper. In his first term, he served in South Korea and Fort Bragg, NC where he was deployed to peacekeeping operations during Restore Democracy / Uphold Peace in Haiti in the early 90's. Upon leaving the military he started college and joined the California National Guard.

Mr. Danyiel has always had a love for the Semitic Languages. He was blessed to be able to pursue his language learning with the military. The California National Guard taught him to be an Arabic Linguist. Shaul Danyiel attended the intensive Arabic Language Program at the Defense Language Institute in the beautiful city of Monterrey, CA. He served as an Arabic translator for the military.

Shaul Danyiel attended one year at Fuller Theological Seminary studying Ancient Near Eastern Languages including Ancient Hebrew, Ugarit, and Koine Greek.

He received his first Rabbinical Ordination as an Independent Rabbi in 2004. He then received an Orthodox Ordination from Rabbi Kellermer in 2007. In 2013, he received Rabbinical Ordination from Rabbi Don Channen as well as a Masters of Rabbinical Studies from Yeshiva Pirchei Shoshanim (YPS).

Rabbi Danyiel has been teaching the Hebrew language at the Language Door language center, and in Synagogues since 2000.

Made in the USA
Columbia, SC
29 September 2018